PRIVATE EQUITY CONCEPTS &TERMS

Copyright © Sameer Jain

Table of Contents

EXECUTIVE SUMMARY

Private equity has become recognized as an asset class that offers potential high returns, somewhat higher risk and diversification from a traditional portfolio of marketable securities. In recognition of these potential benefits, many public funds have adopted investment policies that set forth an allocation to private equity.

Public fund investments have driven a significant amount of the evolution that has occurred over the last two decades. The range, size, and complexity of offerings as well as the number of investors and partnerships have expanded considerably. While the investment merit, reputation and capabilities of general partners are of paramount importance in the decision-making process, private equity contracts have also evolved to become complex agreements and require considerably more attention.

We explore two questions:

1. **Are financial interests aligned between general partners and limited partners?**

2. **Do the ongoing management practices of a partnership represent a continual alignment between general partners and limited partners?**

After a thorough review, it is our opinion that while private equity investors have done much to improve the alignment of interests, however there is much more they can still do to further align interests.

This study addresses these two questions and will help private equity investors develop practices to improve the alignment of their interests with general partners. This study provides:

- an educational medium to raise the level of knowledge of contractual terms and issues that impact financial and ongoing management of partnerships;

- items for consideration when negotiating specific contractual terms.

Our analysis focuses on contractual terms and conditions that impact financial implications to limited partners and terms and conditions that affect the management of the partnership. These are organized into these two principal areas. A third section contains other points for consideration. There are numerous terms and conditions to consider and the study highlights the ones we considered to be valuable. The following financial and managerial terms and conditions were the most important.

Key Financial Terms

We believe that three financial terms should be a focus for investors for the purpose of aligning interests: the **management fee, carried interest and capital commitment by general partners**. Traditional terms of 2% management fee, 20% carried interest and 1% general partner capital commitment are not the status quo anymore. There are significant differences in processes and resources needed for different private equity categories. For example, the effort and expertise required to manage a venture capital partnership is considerably different from that of an LBO partnership. We have found evidence of partnerships, both established and recently formed, that have moved away from traditional terms and toward ones that better align interests financially.

The management fee, expressed as a percent of committed capital, may appear small, but it must be considered along with the amount of capital being raised and the contractual term of the partnership. The resultant absolute dollars in fees over the term of the partnership must be evaluated with respect to the general partners' perceived ability to add value and a "reasonableness" check. There are alternatives to fees based on the percentage of committed capital method that investors should know about. Budget-based fees and sliding fees that ramp up and down over time are two alternative methods described herein.

The carried interest represents a financial alignment of interests. The issue is the split of profits between the general partner and the limited partners. We find that the 20% carried interest to general partners should not be the norm anymore. Investors should negotiate the carried interest in relation to their overall assessment of the partnership, including the size, and other financial terms such as the management fee and capital commitment of the general partner. The general partner capital commitment also needs to be evaluated in monetary terms. In dollars, 1% may be a substantial amount if the partnership is large, or a reasonable amount if the partnership is small. The success of prior funds for a seasoned partnership is an additional factor that needs to be considered. An established general partnership vividly demonstrates its ongoing interests through a meaningful capital commitment.

Key Managerial Terms

Terms that impact the managerial life cycle of a partnership are also important and need to be addressed more extensively by investors. Properly structured financial terms can create strong incentives for general partners to perform, but they are not perfect and can lead to circumstances where effort and desire are diminished. Other events may occur, organizational or even personal, over the partnership term that can impair the general partnership's abilities. The terms that can address and mitigate these potential risks are: **advisory boards, distribution policy, no-fault divorce, termination of general partners, and winding down**.

Advisory boards were perceived with mixed reviews from the groups we surveyed, but we feel that a well-structured and well-run board can add value. Advisory boards should be well defined within the contract with respect to their purpose, responsibilities, and authorities. Investors should also conduct due diligence on the individuals who will be serving as advisory board members.

The distribution policy should specifically address how and when general partners and limited partners receive profits as investments are liquidated. The timing and form of distribution (cash versus securities) also need to be defined in the partnership agreement.

A no-fault divorce term allows limited partners to halt additional capital contributions if there is a loss of confidence in the general partner. No-fault divorce will also create the incentive to get the fund fully invested within an acceptable time frame. No-fault divorce will create pressure, but we feel it is positive pressure at a crucial stage during the investing process.

The ability to terminate individual general partner(s) is an important right that limited partner should demand. This term assures a proper check and balance if the managerial harmony of the general partnership becomes disrupted by a particular general partner.

Wind down provisions address the last stage of a partnership where remaining assets are liquidated and distributed, outstanding liabilities are paid, and any remaining escrows are settled or adjusted. Wind down provisions in use today vary considerably and investors can avoid numerous future problems if these are better defined and structured from the start.

Large investors face additional problems of having to invest considerable sums and being able to manage and administer a reasonable number of relationships. The number of general partners who have demonstrated the ability to deliver strong returns for large commitments is limited. Consequently, large investors may have difficulty negotiating better terms with large general partnerships. This is not a situation that will resolve itself overnight, but it is one that needs to be acknowledged as the supply/demand dynamics that exist today, and these may be different tomorrow. Large investors will continue to push the envelope and express their needs. Responsive investment managers will design products and services to fill them.

In developing the study, we collected the opinions and views of all significant parties involved in private equity investing. We began with a survey of the experiences and attitudes of nine public fund representatives, their respective private equity consultants, and attorneys. The key issues that concerned these groups were highlighted and presented to a group of private equity general partners in a questionnaire. The general partners were asked to respond to these issues and to provide their feedback. While the number of responses might not be considered a statistically significant sample set, the expertise and influential ability of the individuals among the groups sampled are considerable and substantive.

We hope this study sparks a shift in the way investors participate in and think about the private equity markets. Limited partners, by investing 99% of the committed capital of a partnership, have a responsibility to ensure that their interests are protected by having the appropriate terms and conditions. Ultimately, market forces will dictate the economics of supply and demand for private equity, however the dissemination and use of this study among investors, legal counsel, independent third parties, and general partners will challenge "established" thinking and traditions and result in further improvements in the alignment of interests as well as continued growth of the private equity markets.

I. KEY FINANCIAL TERMS

The following are key contractual terms that impact either the direct financial results or the performance evaluation of a partnership:

- Aggregation
- Calculation of Internal Rate of Return
- Capital Commitment of General Partner
- Capital Take-Down Schedules
- Carried Interest
- Cash Versus In-Kind Distribution
- Clawback
- Fees
    - "Traditional" Fees
    - Budgeted Fees
    - Sliding Fee Scales
    - Transaction Fees
- Hurdle Rates
- Performance Benchmarks
    - Absolute Return (Multiple of Money)
    - Cash Flow Adjusted Equity Market Index IRR
    - Vintage Year Comparisons
    - Cash-on-Cash Return

Aggregation

Aggregation or netting is a portfolio view of a partnership. Aggregation is important when computing the carried interest, or profit split of the partnership between general partners and limited partners.

The private equity industry evolved from a deal-by-deal calculation of carried interest to the aggregation method. Previously, the carried interest was based on individual portfolio deals. Deal-by-deal carried interest allows general partners to receive carried interest from profitable deals without being penalized for unprofitable deals. As such, deal-by-deal carried interest can create a temptation for general partners to concentrate on strong performing companies while neglecting mediocre performers. To align the interest of the limited and general partners, deal-by-deal accounting has been virtually eliminated, allowing both the general and limited partners to focus on the aggregate portfolio.

Points for Consideration
We support the industry's move to aggregation because we believe this method represents a better alignment of interests for general partners and limited partners. During periods of strong demand for private equity, some general partners have attempted to get carried interest terms based on a deal-by-deal basis. We recommend that investors not agree to deal-by-deal carried interest terms.

Another good reason to avoid deal-by-deal carried interest is the greater administrative burden to investors from the additional accounting detail. Finally, the standards of fiduciary prudence support a focus on the total portfolio rather than on individual investments.

Calculation of Internal Rate of Return

The net internal rate of return (IRR) is the return received by limited partners that equates the current value of the fund to all the capital contributions into the fund and distributions out of the fund to limited partners. Mathematically, the IRR is the implied discount rate that will make the present value of a stream of cashflows sum to zero:

$$0 = \sum_{i=0}^{N} CF_i (1 + IRR)^{-\left(\frac{n_i}{c}\right)}$$

where,

CF = Net Cashflow = distributions - takedowns in all periods except for the last period where Net Cashflow = Net Asset Value + Distributions - Takedowns

i = the sequence of cashflows

c = the compounding period per year (e.g., 12 for monthly, 4 for quarterly, etc.)

n = the number of periods between the current cashflow and the first cashflow

In practice, the actual IRR calculation and its components may vary considerably. The timing for posting of cash flows as well as the valuation of distributions, especially noncash ones, can have material impact to the IRR that is calculated.

Points for Consideration

Where the general partner's carried interest is dependent on the IRR calculation, it is important for the limited partner to verify the computation. Unless the limited partner has the resources, an independent third party (*e.g.*, a qualified investment consultant) should validate the IRR computation.

The net-IRR definition, that is inclusive of all expenses and fees charged to the partnership, should be used for reporting and evaluating results. The investor should always ask to see the formal definition of the net-IRR. An illustrative example of the computation would also be helpful. Spreadsheet programs such as Microsoft Excel® enable the IRR to be computed easily using the =XIRR( ) function, the amount and dates of cash flows (contributions and distributions) and the current valuation of the limited partner's interests.

An IRR computation assumes that all distributions continue to earn the same return from remaining investments in the partnership. A modified-IRR calculation that reinvests distributions at the rate of return achieved from where the distributions are reinvested will reflect the true returns for the actual investment. Fixed income investors will note that IRR is the same as the yield-to-maturity (YTM) on a bond and that reinvestment risk is the problem of interest income being reinvested at different rates than the YTM. However, the simple IRR appears to be the most widely used method, which allows for some comparability to some benchmarks, and it does not require the assumption of another rate of return for distributions.

We feel it is time for the industry to move toward a standardized method for computing, reporting, and presenting returns. Until that point is reached and perhaps even after, investors should obtain the underlying data used to compute returns and apply a consistent methodology for all their private equity partnership investments.

Capital Commitment of General Partner

The capital commitment of the general partner refers to the financial commitment that the general partner makes to the partnership. This commitment is in addition to the general partner's duties to manage the partnership operations. The Internal Revenue Code and related Revenue Rulings have suggested that the minimum general partner contribution be at least 1%. This is the basis for the industry standard of a 1% capital commitment of general partners.

Some limited partners believe the capital commitment is made solely to comply with federal tax laws. Others perceive the capital commitment of the general partner as representing more than tax law compliance. These limited partners expect it to financially impact the individuals making up the general partnership in a substantial way, thereby enhancing the general partner risk and arguably more closely aligning their interests with the limited partners.

Form of Contribution

The contribution is typically made in cash, although some general partners may seek to make their capital contribution in the form of promissory notes to the fund or to pledge equity from deals already made. General partners may also seek to include their organizational expenses as part of their capital contribution. Limited partner investors overwhelmingly prefer the capital commitment to be paid in cash. Once committed, the capital contribution is subject to the identical take-down schedule as the limited partners' contributions. The general partner is obliged to disclose any changes that have a material adverse effect on the general partner's ability to meet this responsibility.

Level of Commitment

General partners of larger funds ($200 million and over) may seek to make less than a 1% commitment, to the extent permitted by federal tax law, due to the high dollar value of such a contribution. Some limited partners evaluate the significance of the general partner capital commitment. These limited partners perceive the percentage of the partnership and corresponding dollar value as less important than its relative significance to the general partner. There is strong interest among some limited partners that the commitment reflects a meaningful investment relative to the general partner's personal wealth. For this reason, certain limited partners are naturally more attracted to funds with a higher general partner commitment. The difficulty lies in determining the relative level of commitment where the general partner's personal wealth is at risk, since this information is generally not disclosed.

In addition, there is an issue of whether every individual serving as the general partner should personally make a financial commitment to the fund. Within the entity acting as general partner there is a combination of individuals providing financial resources and investment expertise. There are two schools of thought on this issue. Some believe it is sufficient if the entity as a whole supply both financial resources and investment expertise. Others believe that everyone within the general partnership should be required to provide both financial resources and investment expertise.

Many limited partners view the 1% standard as an inadequate sharing of risk, especially in the case of second or third generation funds, where the total capital commitment would be less than 1% when the funds are viewed in aggregate.

Points for Consideration

Clearly, there must be evidence that the general partner commitment has met the requirements of federal tax law. If the purpose of the federal tax law requirement is to protect limited partners, it is not unreasonable to expect the same level of capital commitment for second and third generation funds. Aside from tax issues, the commitment should not diminish with subsequent funds.

In our view, the general partnership entity should provide the required committed capital and the investment and management expertise. It is not necessary to require that everyone contribute to the capital commitment. The important point is that a synergy is created with the general partnership by virtue of whatever the individuals contribute, whether it be financial resources or investment expertise.

There are examples of general partners contributing more than 1%. This has been favorably received by investors. General partners will often participate in limited partnership shares for the excess contribution over 1%. Since limited partners typically receive distributions before general partners do, the risk on the excess contribution is reduced.

However, if the general partner's excess contribution is made as a limited partner, then general partners should be expected to waive their voting rights on these shares.

The portion of personal wealth that the general partner capital commitment represents will be a difficult item to ascertain and we do not feel this is a fruitful avenue to pursue. There are personal attestations made by general partners, but it is unlikely that they will produce personal financial statements to support them. Moreover, analysis of personal financial statements could be a considerable burden without significant benefits.

For established general partnerships, obtaining disclosure of the carried interest received by prior partnerships will provide considerable insight into assessing the relevant importance of the current capital commitment.

Capital Take-Down Schedules

This term describes the schedule used to represent when limited partners required capital contributions.

Traditionally, capital calls were made according to a fixed schedule. Agreements required one-third of the capital at the closing, one-third during the second year and the balance within four years after the closing. Another common method was to call capital in quarters rather than in thirds.

Gradually, general, and limited partners moved to a more flexible approach. The flexibility in the form of more frequent capital calls led to an improvement of IRR. The calculation of IRR begins once the general partner has control of the capital. If the general partner is forced to make the capital call before finding a suitable investment, the IRR will be depressed while the cash is held in short-term money market accounts.

Currently, general partners provide advanced notice within 5-60 days before the capital call. Under this more flexible structure, limited partners may continue to manage their capital at rates that exceed short-term rates until the general partner is ready to make an investment.

Points for Consideration

Our view is that capital should be called on a "just-in-time" or "as needed" basis for two distinct reasons. First, the general partner will only earn cash equivalent rates of return on any idle cash it holds. These rates, when blended with the actual returns of the investments, will result in a lower IRR. It is in both the general and limited partners' interests to structure the capital take-down schedule in a manner that avoids depressing the IRR. Secondly, public funds generally have a low target allocation for liquid assets due to their high levels of cash inflows and relatively predictable cash outflows. Because little is held in cash, the return of the public fund during the period a partnership is investing capital is likely to exceed that of any short-term money market accounts in which the general partner may invest. It is prudent then that assets continue to be managed by the public fund until they are needed by the general partners. If the capital is not invested, then it should be returned immediately less any applicable agreed upon fees.

Carried Interest

Carried interest is the share of the partnership profits received by the general partner. As the general partner's major form of compensation, the carried interest motivates the general partner to achieve the principal investment goals of the limited partners: superior performance, capital appreciation and high profits. Should other forms of income, such as management fees, become a substantial source of general partner compensation, the power of the carried interest to align interests is drastically diminished.

The way carried interest is divided among individuals making up the general partnership is rarely disclosed and is seldom discovered even during due diligence.

The most common carried interest split is 80/20, with 20% of profits going to the general partner. The 80/20 split is attributable to the early years of the private equity industry where a 20% carried interest was a substantial incentive for the general partner's performance.

Most funds implement the 80/20 standard with slightly more variation among non-venture funds than venture funds. Some general partners may agree to receive a lower split to make the fund more attractive to limited partners. Rarely is a general partner's profit share above 20%, although some attempts to increase the carried interest to 25% are being made by general partners with exceptionally strong past performance.

Points for Consideration
Often a major factor influencing the decision to invest in a partnership is the synergy among the individuals making up the general partner entity, therefore, ample justification exists for requiring disclosure about the carried interest division among individuals. It is important that the division of carried interest motivates and rewards valuable individuals appropriately. This division could change over time and disrupt the synergy, therefore a contract provision specifically covering this issue provides more protection rather than a mere disclosure of information during the due diligence stage.

The traditional 80/20 split for carried interest is still the most common arrangement, but we note example differences when combined with nontraditional management fees and general partner capital commitments above 1%. It can be argued that the traditional split is no longer appropriate for large funds. The time, effort and expertise needed to successfully manage a $1 billion fund is probably not 10 times greater than that which is needed to manage a $100 million fund. A more reasonable correlation between time, effort, expertise and profits should be negotiated. The carried interest negotiations should also be evaluated with the management fee in mind. A higher carried interest with a lower management fee may result in a higher net-IRR to limited partners.

In the example on the following page, using the base case assumptions described in section V, a 25% carried interest with a 1.5% management fee would provide a better net-IRR to investors in year 10 than would a 20% carried interest with a 2% management fee. This example also illustrates a second point. If the partnership's expected term is shorter, as might be the case with LBO or mezzanine funds, then it may not be beneficial to increase the carry and lower fees. As shown in years 5 and 6 in the example, the 20% carry/2% fee IRR is better than the 25% carry/1.5% fee IRR. It is important that investors work through the various scenarios and understand the financial implications.

Investors should not rely solely on the numbers the model might suggest. For example, a 15% carry/3% fee scenario might result in better long-term returns if the underlying investments perform well, but a general partner might find less incentive to add value when they are assured a 3% fee.

There are three methods for computing carried interest: aggregation, deal-by-deal, and hurdle rates. With hurdle rates, the carried interest depends on the computation of the IRR and it would be beneficial to have an independent third party verify the IRR when these are used.

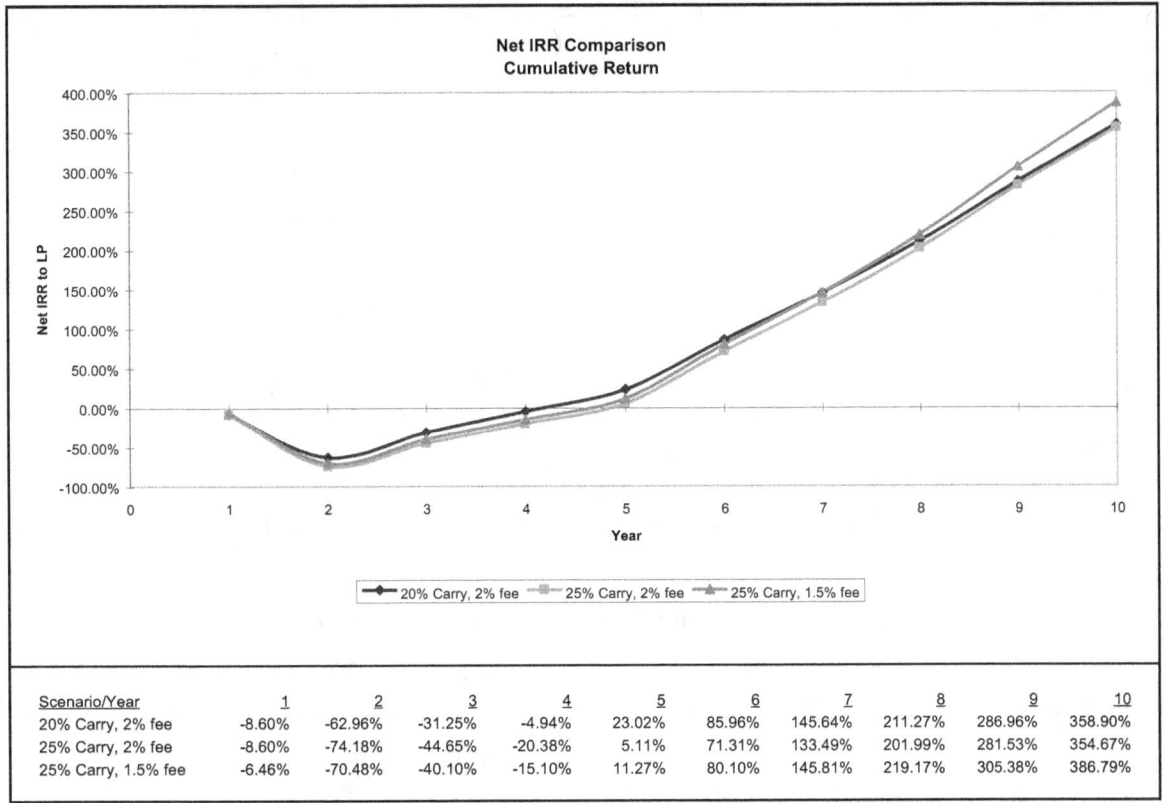

Net IRR Comparison
Cumulative Return

Scenario/Year	1	2	3	4	5	6	7	8	9	10
20% Carry, 2% fee	-8.60%	-62.96%	-31.25%	-4.94%	23.02%	85.96%	145.64%	211.27%	286.96%	358.90%
25% Carry, 2% fee	-8.60%	-74.18%	-44.65%	-20.38%	5.11%	71.31%	133.49%	201.99%	281.53%	354.67%
25% Carry, 1.5% fee	-6.46%	-70.48%	-40.10%	-15.10%	11.27%	80.10%	145.81%	219.17%	305.38%	386.79%

Lastly, it is helpful to consider the expected returns of the underlying portfolio in assessing the management fee/carried interest issue. The example on the following page shows what the net-IRR to a limited partner would be versus 10% to 40% rates of return on the underlying portfolio companies. The effect of changing the management fee from 1% to 2% while at the same time changing the carried interest from 30% to 20% is illustrated. The implication is that if the underlying expected returns of the investments made by the partnership is low, then a low fee/high carry is preferable. If expected investment returns are 20% to 30%, then it still makes sense to have low fee/high carry terms. On the other hand, if portfolio company investment returns are very high (e.g., 40%), then the traditional 2% fee/25% carry term is the better structure, although not significantly better.

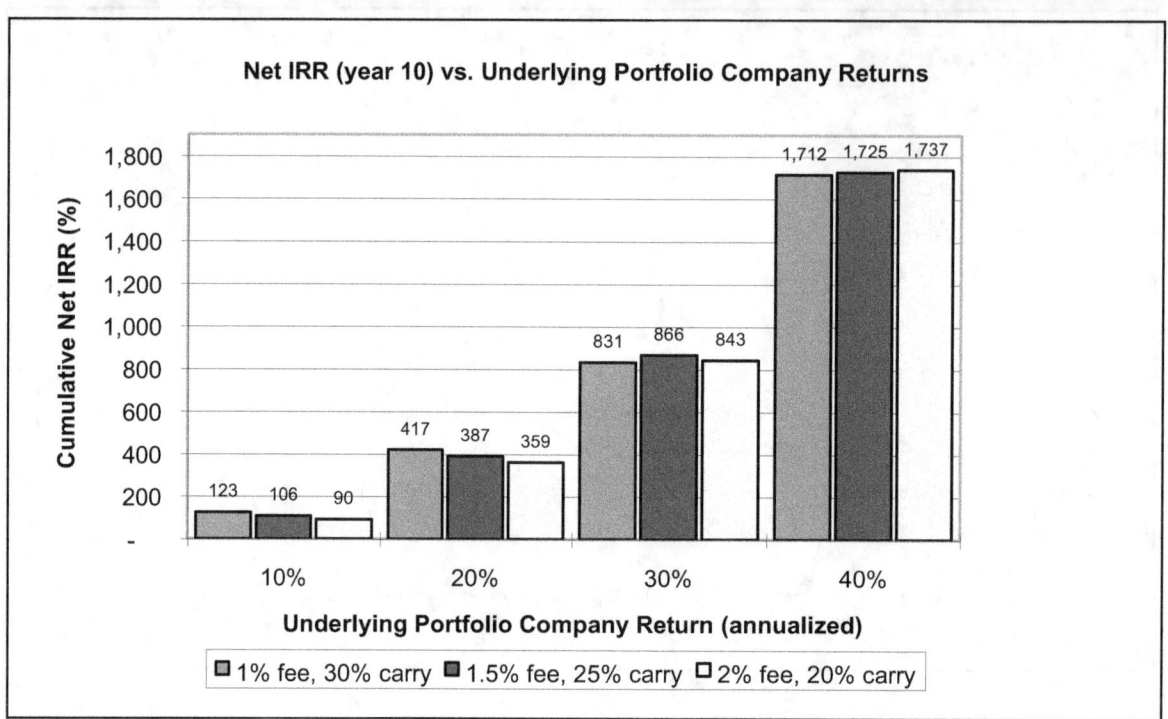

Net IRR (year 10) vs. Underlying Portfolio Company Returns

Cash Versus In-Kind Distribution

Profits are distributed to the limited and general partners either in the form of cash or in the form of securities. The distribution form is defined in all agreements.

Cash distributions have both positive and negative implications for general and limited partners. For the general partner, the positive aspects of a cash distribution include the immediate realization of return, less administrative duties and minimal adverse impacts on stock prices. For the limited partner, the positive aspects of cash distributions also include the immediate realization of return, as well as no responsibility for liquidating securities and no exposure to market volatility.

On the downside, a cash distribution denies the limited partner the benefits of further price increases in the stock. For taxable partners, general or limited partners, cash distributions trigger a tax liability. Distribution in-kind allows the taxable partners to hold the securities and defer the realization of taxable gains.

Certain issues arise with in-kind distributions of restricted securities. A restricted security is a security acquired in a transaction that did not involve a public offering. Under the Securities Act, restricted securities may not be sold without registration with the SEC or without an exemption from registration such as Rule 144. Specifically, Rule 144 applies to sales of stock held for two years after the stock was acquired from the company or an affiliate of the company, and applies to the sale of stock by the affiliate. An affiliate refers to an individual or an entity that directly or indirectly controls a company, which in most cases includes the general partner but excludes limited partners. Therefore, Rule 144 allows restricted securities to be distributed to limited partners without the expense of requiring SEC registration.

Rule 144 restricts the limited partners' ability to resell the restricted securities they received in-kind. Specifically, Rule 144 stock is not available to be sold until 90 days after a company's initial public offering. Volume limitations, manner of sale and notice requirements are also imposed. Regardless of whether the partnership or its partners are affiliates, two-year stock distributed to limited partners will continue to be subject to these liquidation restrictions.

The resale of three-year stock distributions by limited partners who are not affiliates is exempt from the liquidation restrictions of Rule 144. Under Rule 144(k), three-year stocks are eligible for immediate resale by the limited partner. Rule 144(k) permits nonaffiliates, or limited partners, to sell three-year securities with few or none of the foregoing restrictions, making them available to be sold immediately after a company's initial public offering.

With in-kind distributions, valuation methods are set forth in the limited partnership agreement. A commonly used method is to value stocks immediately prior to the day of distribution. A second approach is to value stock according to the average price of the stock over a period of days or weeks before the distribution day.

Points for Consideration
The form of distribution desired by limited partners may differ depending on their tax status. Ideally limited partners should be granted the right to receive cash or securities depending on their preference near the date of distribution as may be permissible under the law. Additionally, nontaxable investors may find it more attractive to join partnerships where most or all of the limited partner investors are also nontaxable entities.

Most of the time nontaxable limited partners are best served by receiving cash or freely tradable securities. Limited partners should not receive two-year Rule 144 stocks due to the trading restrictions related to volume. Receiving stocks under Rule 144 volume limitations puts the limited partners at market risk because of their inability to liquidate the stock immediately.

In addition to stating the types of in-kind securities that are acceptable, agreements must specifically address valuation methods. In partnerships where the limited partners receive an advanced notice of the distribution, the most appropriate valuation method will be one that incorporates an average of the price over a certain number of days. With advance notice, the potential for the information to spread exists and could result in a dramatic decrease in the stock price. Basing valuation on an average that encompasses trading activity after the date of distribution protects the limited partners from a plummeting stock price. Distribution management services are provided by some general partnerships as well as unaffiliated third parties. This might be useful to consider if the limited partner has no internal capability or expertise in managing liquidation of distributed stock. The distribution policy establishes the timing and structures for managing distributions. This is discussed in-depth under Distribution Policy in the Key Managerial Terms section.

Clawbacks

Clawback or "look back" provisions allow for a review of the total profit distribution from the partnership at the end of the term. The purpose of a clawback is to provide assurance that the limited partners have received their capital contribution, the fees they paid and any hurdle rate of return before any carried interest is shared. Additionally, the clawback is a mechanism to recapture overpayments to the general partners if they received more than their stated carried interest. The clawback provision requires return of any excess to the limited partners.

In essence, the clawback provision is a promise to repay limited partners at the end of the term if the general partners somehow received more money than they should have over the life of the partnership. While this is conceptually appealing, implementing this provision and collecting the money owed to limited partners might not be an easy task, especially if individuals in the general partnership have left the partnership, died, or disposed of the money that was distributed to them.

Points for Consideration

An escrow account established to hold a portion of the general partner's carried interest during the life of the fund can provide some assurance that the general partnership will have the ability to reimburse limited partners if the clawback provision is used at the end of the term. An appropriate amount to be held in escrow is 25% or more of the after tax carried interest received by the general partner. Withdrawals from the escrow account prior to termination of the partnership should be limited to payment of any income taxes attributable to interest or other amounts earned by the escrow account.

It may be appropriate to release the escrow account to the general partners and stop requiring additional deposits of carried interest by the general partners if the fund has achieved a return of all capital and a good rate of return (*e.g.*, a return well above the hurdle rate or a high absolute return). However, one further consideration that would argue for maintaining the escrow until the end of the term is that general partners could conceivably receive more than they are entitled to if the disposition of liquidation is such that good performers are sold first and the bad deals remain. The escrow at that point may have been released. The full release of the escrow could be a topic that the advisory board addresses.

In addition to a clawback provision and an escrow account, another level of protection is an audit by an independent, non-investing third party to verify the accuracy of carried interest on a periodic basis. The auditing party should be selected by the advisory board and paid for through the management fee.

Finally, limited partners should ask for joint and several obligations with named individuals personally responsible for repayment of clawbacks in the event of overpayment. This provides flexibility and facilitates collections if necessary.

Fees

"Traditional" Fees

Management fees are necessary to pay for the ongoing operating expenses of the partnership. All investors feel that the management fees should be reasonable to assure the ongoing operation of the partnership. Excessive fees can represent a misalignment of interests. An annuity stream of undue management fees can represent a misalignment of interests by reducing the financial motivation of general partners to achieve high returns.

The "typical" arrangement today for management fees is for a fund to charge an annual fee of 1.5% to 2.5% of total committed capital. In the early 2000s, some funds set fees between 1.5% and 2% of committed capital or net asset value. Venture funds also tended to be smaller and the perception was that fees of 2% or even higher were "appropriate."

Today, some general partners are able to raise buyout funds of over $5 billion. Investors argue that such large size should produce some notable economies of scale and that management fee concessions should be made. Supply and demand factors typically dictate what the management fee will be. If demand for a general partnership is strong, then the management fee tends to be at the high end of the range. Additionally, strong general partners with proven track records tend to be able to command premium fees. However, if market demand is weak, the management fee can often be negotiated, and concessions are often granted for a lead or substantial investor.

Points for Consideration

If a large investor intends to make a substantial investment in a partnership, then fee negotiations may be fruitful. Smaller investors may be able to benefit by using a fund-of-funds, or a discretionary private equity consultant, who will have more negotiating power for its collective clientele than the individual investor will have on its own. New funds or greener general partners are likely to offer fee concessions to raise funds. Negotiations between annual management fee and the carried interest split tend to be an area of trade off. Management fees seldom fall below 1.5% and carried interest to the general partners seldom rises above 25%. Budgeted fees are perceived by many to be an improvement over the traditional flat management fee structure. Additionally, scaled fees are also useful for reflecting the higher level of effort by the general partner during the earlier years of the partnership where the deal-making and due diligence efforts are more intense.

Investors should also try to negotiate carried interest terms that return committed capital and all management fees and expenses before the general partner shares in any profits.

Budgeted Fees

Budgeted fees are management fees determined by the budgeted annual operating expenses of the fund. Typically, an annual budget is presented to the advisory board or limited partners for approval.

Conceptually, this seems to be a method of fees that creates accountability and implies a better alignment of interests. Surprisingly, our survey of the public funds was mixed in this area. Budgeted fees were considered an improvement by some, and others felt that they were a meaningless way to disguise the traditional management fee structures,

because the result would still be a 2% to 2.5% fee.

Points for Consideration

There is no evidence that budgeted fees reduce potential investment returns. However, it is clear that budgeted fees that are less than traditional management fees will enhance returns to the investor. The budgeted fee approach is an application of the cost analysis general partners make when evaluating potential deals and this reflects the same standards.

To minimize potential problems, the process by which budgeted fees are negotiated each year and resolution of any disputes should be formally defined within the partnership agreement.

It should be noted that during periods of high inflation, budgeted fees may result in higher fees. If budgeted fees are used, we recommend a maximum nominal amount be negotiated.

Budgeted fees were viewed very negatively from most general partners we surveyed. Comments included concerns that limited partners would be micromanaging the partnership; negotiating budgets would not be a good use of time; budgets create "cost-plus" thinking; and "our budget is proprietary information." Interestingly, fund-of-funds managers felt that budgeted fees were helpful and their experiences in using them have been positive.

We feel that budgeted fees are an improvement since they create a check and balance system each year that subjects general partners to more accountability, planning and cost control. In essence, this is no different than the disciplines applied by general partners in monitoring and controlling expenses in the investments made by the partnership. A large and successful general partnership entity that has the accounting resources in place should be able to develop and discuss budgets.

A budgeted fee approach also eliminates the need to negotiate changes in the fee when a successor fund is introduced or as the current fund is winding down.

A strong and well-run advisory board is the key to a good budget-making process. Continuity of individuals representing limited partners may be a problem. Over the term of a partnership, it can be expected that most of the individuals having a vested interest in the general partnership will still be there, but individuals representing limited partnership interests of public funds are likely to have a higher rate of turnover. This can create problems in implementing a good budget-making process and should be an important consideration.

If budgeted fees are inappropriate or difficult to negotiate, then the sliding fee scale approach may be better than a traditional percentage flat fee on committed capital.

Sliding Fee Scales

A sliding fee scale is a management fee that varies over the life of the partnership. Typically, these are negotiated fees that attempt to recognize the higher level of due diligence and analysis required during the earlier years as the partnership makes investments. The fees are higher during the earlier years of the partnership and decline over time.

Points for Consideration

Venture capital funds tend to be more resource intensive throughout their lives than LBO funds. Consequently, it would be more appropriate to negotiate sliding fee scales for an LBO fund than for a venture capital fund. Phase-in fees, or fees that first slide up during the earlier years of the fund, level off, then slide down in the later years can also create an appropriate alignment of interests. An example would be 1.5% in the first year, 2% during the second year, 2.5% in years three through five, then a scaling downward of 1.5% in years six and seven,

1% in years eight to ten. A phase-in fee can have a dramatic effect on net returns since the present value impact of a change in fees during the early years is greater than a change in later years. This example is illustrated on the following page compared to a flat fee of 2.5% and 2% per annum. The base case assumptions are listed in section V.

Sliding fee scales are perceived to be an improvement over the traditional management fee structure, however, investors tend to favor budgeted-based fees over sliding fee scales. In general, we concur with this perception, but we would also recommend that investors work through the various fee scenarios before drawing conclusions. The model provided as part of this study should be useful in that process.

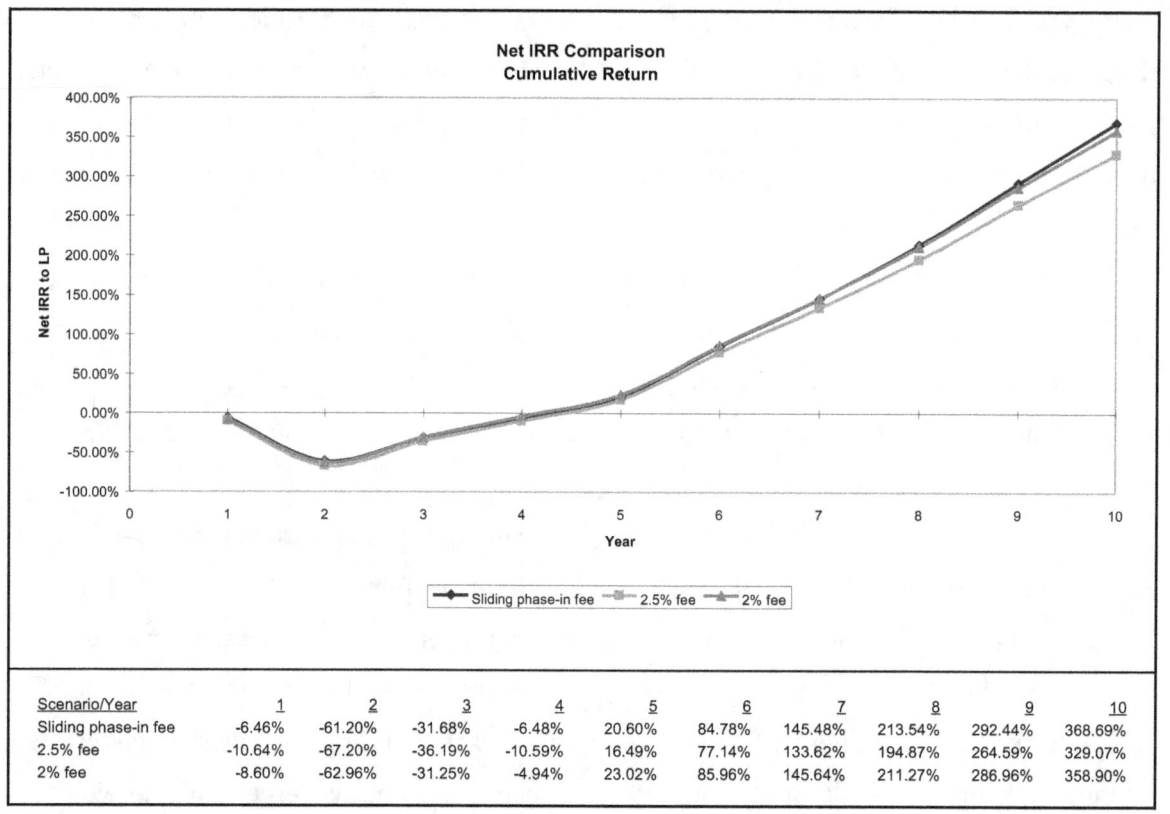

Scenario/Year	1	2	3	4	5	6	7	8	9	10
Sliding phase-in fee	-6.46%	-61.20%	-31.68%	-6.48%	20.60%	84.78%	145.48%	213.54%	292.44%	368.69%
2.5% fee	-10.64%	-67.20%	-36.19%	-10.59%	16.49%	77.14%	133.62%	194.87%	264.59%	329.07%
2% fee	-8.60%	-62.96%	-31.25%	-4.94%	23.02%	85.96%	145.64%	211.27%	286.96%	358.90%

Transaction Fees

Transaction fees are revenues earned from investment banking activities. This includes income received from the work involved in taking a company public through an initial public offering, mergers and acquisitions or the sale of portfolio securities.

In the past, general partners received all transaction fees. Limited partners soon realized that these fees, which could be quite large, were being earned from their investments. The common practice now is for general partners to split transaction fees with limited partners. Transaction fees are typically applied as a reduction to management fees. Payments directly to the partnership incur several tax and legal consequences that most investors do not want to face. Fees for other services, such as consulting or serving as directors, paid to general partners by portfolio companies are usually shared with limited partners in the same manner as transaction fees.

Points for Consideration

Transaction fees can represent a substantial source of income to general partners and a focus on investment banking activities can be a distraction, especially when the partnership is not fully invested. Several general partners, especially venture capital ones, in our survey expressed this view. Some indicated that they do not engage in investment banking activities, or if they did, all transaction fees would be passed on to limited partners. Others provided more favorable splits consistent with the carried interest (80% limited partner/20% general partner) or even the capital contribution (99% limited partner/1% general partner). Most of the LBO funds surveyed took the view that a 50/50 split was appropriate, but a number also acknowledged a trend towards an 80/20 split.

Ideally, an investor would desire 100% of the transaction fees, but this could create an incentive for a general partner to leave money on the table, even if the general partner is the best qualified to perform the task. In our opinion, a 80/20 split, or one consistent with the carried interest split represents a fair apportioning of transaction fees.

Finally, transaction fees should be credited against future management fees or refunding earlier fees to the extent of the sharing arrangement. This will resolve any potential timing differences between management fees paid and transaction fees received.

Hurdle Rates

Most contracts today include a provision referred to as the hurdle, or preferred rate, which requires that the investment achieve a minimum rate of return before the general partnership receives its carried interest. This implies that a return beyond the limited partners' capital contribution must be achieved before the general partner can share in the profitability of the investment. The hurdle rate is intended to align the interests of the general and limited partners by giving the general partner added incentive to outperform a traditional investment benchmark. This is a basic objective of the partnership. Hurdle rates typically range from 5% to 10% and are often tied to a spread over Treasury Bill returns. Hurdle rates have reached as high as 25%.

The calculations of hurdle rates vary. The return may be based on unrealized gains, on realized but undistributed gains, or on distributed cash. If based on distributed cash, distribution can become rather complicated, especially when a clawback is attached to the hurdle rate.

A hurdle rate provision is becoming a standard feature in leveraged buyouts, distressed debt, and mezzanine partnerships. It is found less frequently in early-stage venture capital funds because these investments generally do not produce cash early in the life of the partnership.

Points for Consideration

We support the industry's move toward the use of hurdle rates. General partner's profits should be subordinate to the limited partner's profits. The hurdle rate provision creates a structured subordination that helps align interests. However, it should be noted that there are some problems that may occur when hurdle rates are used.

Establishing an excessive hurdle rate may dampen the positive effect of aligning the interests of the limited and general partners. If a general partner believes they will not make a hurdle rate, they may take on excessive risk or prematurely exit from certain portfolio investments to the detriment of the partnership. During the negotiation process, the general partner may feel justified asking for a higher management fee or better carried interest terms if the hurdle rate is set too high.

Additionally, when there is a clawback with an escrow account, the hurdle rate may create an incentive for the general partner to sell an investment earlier to meet the hurdle rate. When this occurs, the clawback terms are met and the escrow is released to the general partners. One way to alleviate this potential "early sale of winners" is to structure the escrow so that it remains in place until termination or to schedule partial release points.

Performance Benchmarks

An industrywide standard for comparing private equity performance does not presently exist. The illiquid and non-diversified nature of a private equity fund does not lend itself readily to a single benchmark measure. The ultimate return to the investor is the return received after the partnership is finally terminated and all assets are liquidated. However, measuring results during the life of the partnership is important to meet fiduciary responsibilities.

Despite the difficulties for benchmarking, there are various measures being used. The following describes the advantages and disadvantages of each:

Absolute Return (Multiple of Money)

The consensus from our surveys is that a high, double-digit annualized rate of return is the most common benchmark for private equity. General partners are asked what rate of return they expect to achieve over the life of the partnership and this value is then used as an absolute comparative measure.

A "multiple of money" measure is often discussed. This is essentially the cumulative return, such as a tenfold return on investment over the term of the partnership. Achievement of a high annualized rate of return over a long period of time is more impressive than achieving a high annualized rate of return for a short period of time.

In addition to reviewing historical results, prospective investors should ask why a high absolute benchmark return is achievable prospectively and how it is derived. High returns at liquidation occur when a private investment is sold in a public offering. A general partner should be able to articulate the valuation process when a private investment becomes a publicly traded security, when they decide that the time to "go public" is right, and how the valuation process relates to their absolute return benchmark.

A general partner should be asked to discuss how they expect to achieve the absolute benchmark return for a portfolio of investments. Their management of a situation where an investment went bad and the impact on the management of the remaining investments are also important issues to discuss.

Cash Flow Adjusted Equity Market Index IRR

This approach takes the cash inflows and outflows of a partnership and applies it to an equity index such as the S&P 500. Quite often a spread, of the S&P 500 return +5%, is used. The internal rate of return is then computed for this index and compared to the IRR of the partnership.

This measure addresses the question of what the returns would be if the investment of private equity money were invested in another asset class. The shortcoming of this approach is that it doesn't provide a relative comparison within the private equity asset class.

The time-weighted-rate-of-return (TWRR) approach, which excludes the effect of cash flows, is inappropriate since private equity is not priced on a mark-to-market basis.

Vintage Year Comparisons

The vintage year methodology reflects the results of partnerships that were closed in a specific year and their subsequent investment returns. In concept, this methodology helps compare partnerships that are competing from the same starting point in time. As partnerships are investing during the early years, operational costs tend to be very high relative to any payback. This results in a period of low returns before high returns are achieved (the J-curve effect). The vintage year methodology for benchmarking helps to create a more relative comparison, especially during the earlier years of the partnership.

The vintage year approach appears to make the most sense as a relative benchmark. The relative comparison can be improved further by considering funds with the same sector and geographical focus in addition to being from the same vintage year.

While the vintage year benchmark approach can be especially useful, there are some problems:

- There is a sample bias in the average fund size that has occurred over time. The average fund has grown significantly over time. This reflects the impact of large public funds becoming a dominant force in the private equity market.

- The sample size may be limited. This can result in narrow comparisons, for meaningful comparison.

- Terms and conditions vary across partnerships and they change over time. Terms such as fees and take-down schedules have a considerable impact on IRRs.

- Valuations of nonliquidated investments are the subjective judgments of the funds reporting and are not independently verified.

Cash-on-Cash Return

The cash-on-cash return helps to measure a general partner's effectiveness in liquidating portfolio companies. The cash-on-cash return is measured by computing the ratio of cumulative distributions to paid-in (funded) capital. This ratio can be useful for comparing partnerships from the same inception period.

A related measure is the ratio of total partnership value created to paid-in capital. Total partnership value created is equal to the sum of cumulative distributions and current value of the partnership. The current value of the partnership is not a market value, so this ratio is not as clean as the cash-on-cash return.

II. KEY MANAGERIAL TERMS

The following terms are important for investors in the due diligence, ongoing management, and winding down of a partnership:

- Advisory Boards

- Co-Investment

- Conflicts of Interest

- Defaulting Limited Partner

- Disclosure Information

- Distribution Policy

- Indemnification

- Key-Man

- Most Favored Nations Clause

- No-Fault Divorce

- Number of Multiple Funds Being Raised

- Subsequent Closing

- Term

- Termination of General Partner

- UBTI

- Vesting Schedules for General Partners

- Winding Down the Partnership

Advisory Boards

Function

The primary functions of an advisory board are to approve valuations of investments made by the partnership and to address conflicts of interest. Boards may also approve distributions, review operating budgets, assure that annual audits are conducted, reviews the results of these audits, authorize any needed exemptions from partnership covenants, and, when necessary, terminate a general partner. Advisory boards can act efficiently on matters that would otherwise be unmanageable if responses from all limited partners were needed. Those individuals serving on advisory boards do not act as agents for other limited partners investing in the partnership. To properly fill the role of an agent for the limited partners would require a substantial time commitment. An agency relationship would create liability beyond their investment for a trust fund that mistakenly represents the views of other limited partners.

Membership

Limited partnership agreements typically indicate that the general partner will appoint an advisory board. Although a standard approach to determining the members of the board does not exist, most are composed of three to nine representatives of the largest limited partners. General partners may serve as board members; however, they are denied all voting rights. In most cases, board members are not compensated. The public fund representatives we surveyed indicated a preference for named individuals, who are recognized experts, to be represented on the advisory boards rather than unspecified representatives from the entities investing as limited partners.

There are examples of advisory boards made up exclusively of non-investors or in addition to limited partner investors. The general partner's rationale for including non-investors is to benefit from the insights and expertise of various industry experts.

Influence of the Board

The influence of the advisory board is restricted by the legal nature of the partnership that prohibits limited partners from playing an active role in investment decisions. The board's input with regard to investments is strictly advisory and nondiscretionary. The ultimate decisions are made by the general partner. As fiduciaries of trust fund assets, the limited partner investors must react to problems when they occur but cannot be involved with any decision-making that would arguably create liability beyond their capital commitment.

The potential for liability beyond committed capital worries many limited partners. In addition, some limited partners believe advisory boards are overly time-consuming for both the members and the general partner. Because of the debate over the value added by an advisory board, the practice varies. Some partnerships rely heavily on their advisory boards while others do not.

Points for Consideration

A well-functioning advisory board of sophisticated representatives of limited partners is capable of appropriately aligning the interests of the limited and general partners. Although it is not often the practice, it is strongly recommended that the role of the advisory board, their powers and activities be specifically set forth in the investment agreement. The agreement should also state that the individuals serving on the advisory board are not agents for the limited partners. Provisions that state that the general partner will appoint the members of the advisory board should be expanded to

include an explanation of the circumstances where a change will be made in the composition of the advisory board.

Alignment of interests is achieved when the duties of the advisory board are explicitly outlined to include tasks that benefit the partnership, such as reviewing budgets and resolving conflicts of interest. Advisory board duties should specifically exclude any role in the investment decision-making process that would trigger unlimited liability.

The board should meet on an annual or semi-annual basis. It should also be able to promptly convene meetings should serious issues arise that require immediate attention. Superfluous meetings are best avoided because they take valuable time away from the general partners. Issues discussed during advisory board meetings need to be documented and distributed to all limited partners. In addition to keeping limited partners informed, documentation will serve as a check that the advisory board is functioning in the most appropriate and effective manner.

Serving on an advisory board is not a mandatory obligation, however it can provide the investor with better access to information regarding the general partner's activities and the partnership. To protect the advisory board member from additional risk, a partnership should provide indemnification.

Co-Investment

Direct co-investment occurs when the general partners or limited partners invest in entities that have received funds by the partnership. Crossover co-investment occurs when a partnership subsequently invests in companies that have already received money from general partners affiliated with the partnership.

"Cherry picking" is a direct co-investment issue where general partners as individual investors may have the right, but not the obligation, to co-invest in deals made by the partnership. Cherry picking can result in a misalignment of interests as the general partner, with better knowledge of deals, will focus on deals that are more attractive. Riskier investments may end up being financed by the partnership.

Conflicts of interest can also arise if a co-investment is not made in the same type of security, with the same ownership rights, risks and returns. An example would be if a general partner co-invested in a company and received senior debt, while the partnership received unsecured equity.

A second direct co-investment issue is exclusive or nonexclusive co-investment rights granted to limited partners. In practice, there has been little restriction placed on limited partner co-investment.

Crossover co-investment can also be subject to abuse. If, however, crossover co-investment is structured properly to align interests, there can be good upside since it is presumed that the general partner has developed a better understanding of the company and its potential.

Points for Consideration
Limited partners should consider restricting general partner co-investment altogether or allow it only on a *pari passu* basis. Co-investment on a *pari passu* basis means that the general partner is allowed to co-invest, but only if they invest in all of the partnership's investments at the same pro rata basis, at the same time and in the same form. The partnership agreement should not allow the general partner to co-invest on terms more favorable than those offered to the partnership.

Limited partners should be allowed to co-invest, but only after the partnership has met its desired allocation.

Some investors want a partnership to focus on deals that it can do only within its own capital capacity. To those investors, significant co-investment by limited partners may be a concern that the partnership is pursuing investments beyond its level of resources. Other investors find co-investing attractive and actively seek out partnerships where this is possible.

The partnership agreement should require the general partner to disclose to limited partners of any co-investments.

If crossover co-investment is permitted, we suggest the following: an objective, unaffiliated third-party investor determines the price for the additional investment; the additional investment is not done to bail out a problematic situation; the additional investment is not made to allow a general partner or affiliated investor to exit; and the advisory board approves the crossover co-investment.

Conflicts of Interest

Numerous conflicts of interest can potentially exist in any venture capital or LBO investment. A conflict exists when the general partners or those affiliated with the general partner, such as family members or business associates, have personal financial goals that may be different from the goals of the limited partners.

The conflicts causing the most concern arise when the general partners intend to invest the fund in an entity where they personally have a financial interest. Their interest may have been acquired as an individual investor or it may have been acquired by virtue of their position as a limited or general partner in a previous fund.

It is common for limited partnership agreements to address these concerns. Some agreements forbid any investment in entities where the general partners have any financial interest. In other agreements the amount of financial interest must be considered substantial in order to create a conflict. Agreements often provide that such conflicts must be reviewed with the Advisory Board. Investors should be concerned if agreements allow general partners to make such investments first and then provide disclosure to the limited partners after the action.

Most often, investment opportunities appearing to raise the conflicts of interest issue are not automatically excluded but are examined and tested in some way to assure the limited partners that regardless of the conflict, the investment opportunity is still a prudent one. One way to verify the investment prudence is to allow the investment if another unrelated, high quality investor or fund is also making a simultaneous investment. Another way, as previously discussed, is to have the Advisory Board review the matter.

Points for Consideration
We believe that conflicts of interest is one of the most important issues to address in limited partnership agreements. The definition of a conflict of interest should be broadly defined even though the decisions resolving the conflict may be more lenient than strict. Virtually any financial tie to an entity, no matter how insubstantial it may arguably be, no matter how it was acquired and no matter whether it is the general partner or an affiliate of the general partner who has

the financial interest, should be promptly disclosed to all limited partners. If waivers of conflicts of interest are given by the limited partners they should be in writing and contain the limited partners' understanding of the breadth and depth of the conflict as well as a brief description of its rationale for waiving the conflict. This approach protects the limited partners from undesirable actions by the general partner. It also protects limited partners from public criticism should one of the unprofitable investments involving a conflict of interest receive wide public attention.

We do not recommend the preapproval of investment opportunities where conflicts of interest exist, such as an agreement that would specify that an insubstantial financial interest would not be considered a conflict. Additionally, we do not agree that a conflict should be overridden if another investor validates the "prudence" of the investment. This approach establishes a less than deliberate delegation of authority to another unspecified party and can be easily manipulated. A principal role of an advisory board is to address conflicts of interest. This statement and procedures for resolution of conflicts of interest should be included in the partnership agreement.

Defaulting Limited Partner

This provision in partnership agreements relates to the situation of a limited partner who fails to make full payment of its capital contribution when due. It may also refer to a situation where most limited partners elect not to pay the partnership any amount of their commitments because of serious problems with the general partner's performance. This provision is of most concern to the non-defaulting limited partners who do not want their ongoing rights or returns impaired. It may also be of concern to investors who are forced to exit the partnership before the end of its term.

Limited partnership agreements usually give the general partner wide discretion to take action to enable the partnership to make the investment when the defaulting limited partner's contribution was required. The actions may include waiving the default, bringing legal action against the defaulting partner, borrowing money from a commercial bank, offering any non-defaulting limited partner the interest, admitting new limited partners, offering the interest to the non-defaulting limited partners on a pro rata basis or assuming the interest itself. In some cases, the advisory board must concur with the alternative chosen by the general partner.

Points for Consideration

The focus of most investors should be on protecting their rights should another investor default. The limited partnership should be reviewed with that in mind. For example, if a general partner is given the right to borrow money to cure the default of a limited partner, it is important that such borrowing not produce unrelated business taxable income (UBTI) to the other limited partners who may be concerned about taxation. If a general partner decides to assume the limited partner interest itself, it may be important to clarify what the voting rights will be. If the limited partner interest is offered to outsiders, it may be important to specify that such an offering be on the same terms and conditions as the original limited partner interests.

In the rare situation that the investors believe they might need to exit the partnership early, the exit penalties should be well understood. One of the reasons for early exiting may be that a state, local or federal law would make the continuing investment an illegal activity.

Such would be the case if certain social legislation were passed requiring divestment from certain businesses. Another example is if certain limits are initiated under Federal Communications Commission (FCC) regulations because the investor has an aggregate investment in communications businesses in a geographic area that exceeds federal limits.

Disclosure Information

General partners are typically asked to disclose information that provides insight into their commitment of capital and about any potential conflicts of interest or activities that might reduce or impair their ability to manage the partnership prudently.

Most investors are comfortable in asking questions during the due diligence phase that relate to:

- Time commitments to other business activities;
- Employment with other entities;
- Board directorships;
- Past or pending business litigation in which the general partner is involved; and
- SEC violations.

Some public fund representatives indicated it would be helpful to have information regarding:

- Capital commitment as a percentage of personal net worth;
- Capital commitment as a percentage of carried interest gains from prior funds;

- Personal litigation;
- Physical health of key individuals; and
- Executive compensation package for general partners.

Points for Consideration

Some disclosures we believe are important include:

- Other commitments;
- IRS determinations/collections;
- Other legal issues affecting the general partners;
- Financial ties between the partnership and members of the general partners' families;
- Succession plan of general partners;
- Linkage of vesting schedules of general partners to term of the fund;
- Financial statements for the general partnership entity;
- Projected operating budget; and
- Side letter agreements negotiated with other investors.

In considering the disclosures which affect investment decisions, limited partners should decide what disclosed items are important to them throughout the term of the partnership. These items should be included in the agreement.

Distribution Policy

In a broad sense, the term "distribution" relates to how both the general and limited partners receive profits as the investments are liquidated. Usually, the general partner does not begin receiving its share of the profits until an amount equal to committed capital and management fees is returned to the limited partners. In a few situations, distribution to the general partner has occurred after the committed capital was recovered without regard to the recovery of management fees.

The timing of distributions is another part of this issue. Three variations exist. One where both general and limited partners receive profits at the same time. Another is when limited partners share profits on a predetermined date. The third is when the general partner's share is held in escrow until certain conditions are met. The general partner share may be held in escrow to ensure liquidation decisions are properly made. Carefully drafted escrow agreements result in little confusion or controversy over when the general partners are to receive their distribution. In some instances, ambiguous escrow agreements have resulted in unexpected difficulties for the limited partner.

Points for Consideration

In our view, limited partners should recover an amount equal to their capital commitment and share of management fees before the general partners' profit. Secondly, distribution should be made as profits become available, even though this may be inconvenient for general partners who may prefer to make distributions on a predetermined date.

Standardized escrow account agreements should precisely dictate what types of withdrawals may be made, to whom, and under what conditions the escrow account can be released to the general partnership. This will decrease the negotiation time and increase the confidence level of investors.

The form of distribution also affects an investor returns considerably. A more detailed discussion of this is provided under Cash versus In-Kind Distribution in the Key Financial Terms section.

Indemnification

Indemnification provisions in limited partnership agreements are often lengthy, complicated, and best handled by legal counsel. Essentially, they seek to protect the general partners from personal liability or loss arising out of their activities in conducting partnership business. In some instances, indemnification covers limited partners as well, such as when they serve on advisory boards.

Basically, general partners do not want to assume liability unless their actions are grossly negligent. The limited partners usually try to negotiate general partner liability for simple negligence, however, they are not often successful in obtaining this standard. Gross negligence is the intentional failure to perform their duties in reckless disregard of the consequences affecting others. Simple negligence is based on fact that one ought to have known the consequences of his or her acts.

Rarely, do limited partnership agreements recognize different standards of care for the general partners depending upon the specific activity that they are engaged. For example, a general partner's standard of care in selecting and evaluating portfolio companies to be acquired may be different from that general partner's conduct in serving on the board or as an advisor to the portfolio company.

The limited partner's obligation to commit capital to fund the indemnification is usually specified in the agreements. Most often, the limited partner's commitment is limited to their capital contribution and past and future distributions. Sometimes the obligation to pay for the indemnification lasts well beyond the term of the partnership and can be problematic for the limited partner to pay.

Often woven into indemnification clauses are exculpation or "hold harmless" language. These are meant to clear the general partners from fault or blame should negative outcomes with the partnership occur. This language has no meaningful effect.

Points for Consideration
We believe that indemnification provided for the general partner and limited partners serving on the advisory board should be parallel as much as possible.

We also believe that general partners should be held to a high standard of care when they are acting as fiduciaries for limited partners in evaluating and selecting portfolio investments. If a lower standard of care is to be accepted, it should only relate to those activities where the general partner is serving in some capacity with the portfolio company and the basic business judgment rule applies. That rule will protect the general partners if their actions are reasonable and in good faith. The basic business judgment rule is a lower standard than that required of fiduciaries.

General partners who adopt a simple negligence standard expose themselves to more risk, but in doing so they also send forth a strong message that might give investors added confidence that their interests are better aligned.

Key-Man

Key-man provisions address the limited partners' concern for potential turnover of certain named individuals within the general partnership or the retention of a specified percentage of original general partners.

Partnership agreements typically define the allowable actions limited partners may take when faced with general partner turnover. The turnover may be described as one specific person ceasing to devote the necessary business time to the partnership. It may also be described as a combination of key people no longer being active in the management of the fund. Finally, an agreement may specify a certain percentage, or number of persons leaving the partnership, as the turnover justifying limited partner actions. The agreements usually regard the reason for the turnover, whether voluntary or involuntary, as irrelevant.

Limited partnership agreements commonly include a provision outlining the rights of limited partners when the stated turnover occurs. Typically, the limited partners may either exercise their right to have the general partners terminate the partnership, or they may exercise their right to cease any further capital commitments. The latter is more prevalent. Within this provision, the level of agreement among voting limited partners needed before any action can be taken, is usually stated.

When key-man provisions are triggered, a vote among the limited partners is often required. When the limited partners have no obligation to make further capital commitment, no vote may be required. However, when the limited partners are given the right to request the general partner to terminate the partnership, a majority, or more often, a super majority vote is required.

The inclusion of key-man clauses is on the rise in recent years. Many investors seek this provision in all their partnerships agreements. Others demand the clause only when they believe one or two people are critical to the success of the fund.

Points for Consideration
We believe it is important that the key-man provisions be consistent among all limited partners. We would be concerned if side letters existed that have the potential to allow one limited partner to exercise certain rights to the detriment of other limited partners.

Despite the obvious upside to including a key-man provision, it should be noted that when the provision seeks to retain certain individuals within the general partnerships there may be potential for problems. It is desired or expected that a synergy exists among the individuals making up the general partnership. However, when one is considered a key-man, and another is not the synergy could be disrupted.

Most Favored Nations Clause

The most favored nations clause is often requested by large investors to assure that they always receive the most preferential treatment among investors with a fund. This clause assures that any side agreements negotiated by other investors will be received by the investor with the most favored nation clause.

Points for Consideration

Most general partners state that they tend to treat their limited partners as equals, however the reality is that limited partners with more capital to invest are likely to receive greater attention during the fund-raising process. Most general partners also tend to disclose all side agreements as part of the closing package of documents before the fund closing. There should be ample time to review these side agreements and comment or to act on them. Additionally, a situation may arise in the future where a preferential benefit to the limited partner who received a side agreement pertaining to that situation. A properly constructed most favored nations clause that always addresses most preferential treatment during the life of the partnership should provide assurance.

No-Fault Divorce

A no-fault divorce clause is essentially a right to call for a vote of confidence at any time during the life of the partnership. The no-fault divorce clause stipulates the conditions where limited partners may stop contributing capital to the partnership or even terminate the partnership. A no-fault divorce clause typically states that if a specified majority (typically a super majority of those providing 75% or more of the committed capital) of the limited partners decide that they do not want to stay invested in the partnership, they can withhold additional capital take-downs. A no-fault divorce clause that results in termination of the partnership is rare. When it occurs, it is usually linked to fraud and grossly negligent actions of the general partner. Most general partners prefer that in the event of misconduct, a replacement of the irresponsible individuals occurs rather than early termination of the partnership.

The no-fault divorce clause is not new. Larger institutional investors demand it, depending on the situation.

Points for Consideration

No-fault divorce is one of the most difficult clauses for limited partners to negotiate. General partners, especially established ones, are reluctant to grant no-fault divorce since it can impair the partnership's long-term investment strategy.

A no-fault divorce clause for termination is of limited value if the partnership is nearly fully invested. It is probably better in that case to vote for the replacement or addition of a general partner.

Number of Multiple Funds Being Raised

This issue relates to the distraction of attention and resources away from the partnership when the general partners are raising capital for more than one fund at a time. Marketing efforts and raising capital are distractions from the fund that may lead to additional revenue for the general partner and future limited partners but do little to help limited partners in existing funds. Additionally, efforts to get the new capital invested can dilute the resources previously focused on the existing partnership investments.

Most limited partners ask for measures that prevent, limit, or restrict the timing of successive fundraising by the general partner because they want the general partner's undivided attention to the fund where they presently participate. However, a general partner wants to sustain an ongoing business operation, diversify investment risks through successive investment funds, grow revenues and have a greater potential for success. These interests are rational and cannot be averted. Limited partners often negotiate limitations on the number of multiple funds that will be raised and the timing of when additional funds will be raised.

Points for Consideration
At minimum, limited partners should require that no multiple funds be raised until the current fund has reached a point of being fully invested or close to fully invested (two-thirds to three-quarters invested). Agreements should specify dedication of time standards for the general partners to assure that the partnership is receiving proper attention.

On the positive side of this issue, limited partners can also negotiate for rights of first refusal to participate in successive funds.

It may be wise to have the advisory board address limitations on the number of multiple funds the general partnership can actively manage. The advisory board meetings should be used to address the potential conflict of multiple funds, but not be used as a forum for the general partner to market the rolling out of a new fund.

Subsequent Closing

Both general and limited partners would prefer to have one single closing, but many funds tend to have an initial closing followed by subsequent closings. Early investors feel that subsequent investors benefit unfairly by having a shorter at-risk period and are not penalized for being a later-stage investor.

Points for Consideration

Once the first closing is achieved, general partners should remain focused on starting the investment process. Subsequent closings should occur within a reasonable period, no longer than six to nine months. To maintain the proper focus on deal size and scope, the amount of additional capital raised should not exceed a reasonable amount. Subsequent closing terms should reflect these suggestions.

Term

The life of a partnership is typically ten years. Extensions of typically two or three years may be granted upon approval of the advisory board or most of the limited partners. Ten years is generally accepted for venture capital partnerships where the life cycle of investing, managing and liquidating a portfolio is fairly long. LBO partnerships typically receive positive cash flow from their portfolio investments during earlier years. Many LBO partnerships are established entities and use efficient means for finding and bidding investments. As a result, the term for LBO partnerships may be shorter than the norm of ten years for venture partnerships.

Points for Consideration

It is to the benefit of the limited partners to have a shorter term versus a longer one. A shorter term lowers the risk and creates a greater emphasis on the exit strategy where the greatest returns are realized. In certain industries such as computer software, the lifecycle can be noticeably short due to greater efficiencies in product development and distribution as well as a continually active IPO market in this industry. A prospective investor should address the industry dynamics of the underlying investments that will be considered when addressing the term of the agreement. Additionally, the investor should look to the prior experience of a general partner for their actual term experience (*e.g.*, the percentage of liquidated and fully written down investments over time compared to the stated contractual term).

Termination of General Partner

The termination of a general partner becomes an issue when an individual voluntarily withdraws or is removed from the general partnership. In the case of a voluntary withdrawal, death or incapacity, the protections limited partners may need are set forth in the key-man provision in this study. Limited partnership agreements usually provide that a general partner may be removed for "cause" if that is the preference of a majority or supermajority of the limited partners. The necessary vote for removal is typically in the 75% to 90% range. Some agreements state that the vote can be as low as 66% of the independent limited partners. In other agreements the removal of the general partner requires a majority vote of the advisory board. Whether the remaining partners assume the departing partner's interest and liability or whether a substitute general partner is selected is also specified in the agreement. The definition of "cause" varies from agreement to agreement. Basically, the negotiations surrounding this point begin with the limited partner defining "cause" as a breach of fiduciary duties and the general partner defining "cause" as willful, wanton or criminal behavior. Workable definitions of cause include "a substantial breach in the general partner's obligations under the Partnership Act or the agreement" or "a determination by an independent and reasonable fact finder that the general partner is disabled or has breached the agreement in a manner that is material to the partnership." If the removal vote is challenged, some agreements provide for arbitration.

Points for Consideration

Private equity investments, by their very nature, are less liquid than other types of investments public entities make and therefore, the ability to terminate a general partner becomes of great importance. Limited partnership agreements vary substantially in the rights provided to limited partners to force a general partner to leave the partnership. The ability to replace a general partner may be the single most important right of the limited partner. Therefore, the circumstances where this right can be exercised should be carefully negotiated. It should be noted that if a Limited Liability Company (LLC) structure is used for the investment, the removal of the manager is much easier than the removal of a general partner because removal does not need to be based on "cause."

UBTI

A concern for some limited partners is the generation of Unrelated Business Taxable Income (UBTI) under the federal tax code. Public funds, who are usually unaffected by income tax on their investments, are arguably subject to taxation if their investment activity appears to be running a business rather than passively investing in a business.

Public funds concerned about UBTI are the ones that believe their tax favorable status as a "qualified plan" stems from the specific authority in Section 401(a) of the Internal Revenue Codes. To claim such status under this particular code section also means that the UBTI provisions of Section 514 apply to the fund's operations. If a particular investment triggers UBTI, the consequence is that tax is due on the taxable portion of income of that particular investment. It does not mean that all the income generating assets of the entire trust fund are subject to taxation.

Some funds believe that UBTI is not a concern for them because they rely on Section 115 of the Internal Revenue Code, rather than Section 401(a) for their tax favorable status. This is essentially a Constitutional position that public

pension funds are an integral part of a state or local government's essential operations and, as such, the federal government has no authority to tax the states. If a fund claims its tax favorable status under Section 115, the UBTI laws found in Section 514 have no application.

Most limited partners believe that the general partners should use their "best efforts" to avoid investments that would trigger UBTI. Sometimes advisory boards are asked to consider special situations and lessen the best efforts standard when a particularly attractive opportunity is being considered by the general partners.

To date, we know of no public fund that has been audited or forced to pay taxes on investments due to UBTI.

Points for Consideration
We believe there are valid reasons for avoiding UBTI. First, the return to the limited partners is unacceptable because of the taxation. Second, the limited partners believe that any recognition of taxable income may trigger an audit of their other investments or possibly its benefits structure in the case of a public retirement system.

If certain limited partners serving on an advisory board are asked to essentially waive the UBTI avoidance language in the limited partnership agreement, it is important for them to remember that different levels of sensitivity exist among those limited partners not serving on the advisory board. Some care should be taken to see that all views are taken into consideration in this situation.

Situations can arise where general partners find an investment opportunity that by its very nature, or in its present structure, has the potential to cause UBTI. A close examination needs to be made of the costs and benefits of restructuring the acquisition to avoid UBTI.

It should clearly be understood by all parties that some profitable investments may be foregone if any limited partner requires that UBTI be avoided. Those limited partners who are not concerned about UBTI may not be pleased with such restrictions being placed on the general partners. We recommend that special attention be given to this possible scenario and that it be specifically addressed in the limited partnership agreement.

Vesting Schedules for General Partners

The vesting schedule refers to the period from fund start-up date that partners of the general partnership are eligible to receive their share of the carried interest. While conducting due diligence, potential investors should ask to examine the general partnership agreement. In practice, vesting percentages tend to be on average about 20% after one year; 35% after two years and 85% after five years. On average, partners are fully vested after about six years.

Points for Consideration

Since the stated term of a partnership is usually ten years, it is sensible to request alignment of vesting schedules to the term of the partnership or until winding down of the partnership, whichever occurs first. Additionally, the vesting percent over time can be slowed to better reflect the ten-year term. Including the vesting schedules in the limited partnership agreement can be an ideal way to ensure that this alignment is established. Vesting schedules are normally addressed only in the general partnership agreement. The partnership agreement should require consent of the advisory board before changes to vesting schedules can be made.

Winding Down the Partnership

Winding down provisions refer to the process of liquidating all remaining assets in the partnership at the end of the term or the effective date of dissolution. These provisions should address the process for payment of all creditors of the partnership and distribution of remaining proceeds or assets in the partnership. Agreements usually stipulate that winding down expenses will be charged to the partnership.

Points for Consideration

It is important that the winding down process is efficiently and effectively managed. During the winding down period, the general partner's attention is diverted elsewhere. It is likely that the full effort of the general partner will not be on winding down the partnership. A stipulation of a maximum time period for the winding down and termination of the partnership with a financial incentive or penalty would be beneficial in assuring that the process is completed within a reasonable time frame.

Distribution and valuation of assets that cannot be liquidated need to be addressed within the wind down provisions. Distributions-in-kind for certain assets may create problems for some investors depending on their tax or legal status. A process for handling these assets and their eventual liquidation also need to be addressed.

The wind down provision should also set forth the terms for which any reserves or escrow accounts might need to be established or released during the winding down process. Finally, the winding down provisions should also address how a liquidator will be selected if there is no general partner. A simple majority vote of the limited partners or the advisory board should suffice.

III. OTHER POINTS FOR CONSIDERATION

Alternative Investment Structures

The predominant investment structure for private equity investment is the limited partnership. The named general partner entity in the partnership tends to be either a limited liability entity such as a corporation, limited liability corporation or a limited partner. While individuals were named general partners in the early years of private equity investing, an individual named as a general partner is nonexistent today. This two-tiered general partner structure serves to insulate individuals from general liability. Partnerships are preferred investment structures because of their ability to accommodate both pension and non-pension investors, favorable tax treatment, well-established legal precedent and familiarity. Two alternative investment structures, a commingled trust and a limited liability company are discussed below.

Commingled Trust

A commingled trust accommodates qualified, non-taxable investors such as ERISA and public funds. A commingled trust does not require a general partner. An investment advisor manages the trust on a fully discretionary basis and charges a management fee in addition to any fees charged by the underlying partnership investments in the trust.

Commingled trusts are often used by fund-of-funds private equity managers. In addition to private equity partnerships, the commingled trust may have flexibility to invest in direct private companies, post-venture public stocks and small capitalization public stocks.

Fund-of-funds commingled trusts are useful for smaller investors to establish a more diversified private equity allocation than they could making individual limited partnership investments. Additionally, the required private equity expertise is delegated to an external manager. Another advantage of a commingled trust is the sheltering of the investor from investments that may produce UBTI. Investors in a commingled trust receive protection from tax return filing requirements since the trust is responsible for filing and paying taxes on UBTI.

Limited Liability Company

A limited liability company (LLC) is an alternative structure to a limited partnership and may be useful to some public funds in their private equity investments. It is often described as a hybrid between a corporation and a partnership because it offers limited liability like a corporation and single taxation on income like a partnership. In theory, it offers the best of both worlds.

The first LLC statute was enacted in Wyoming in 1977. It was not until 1988 when the IRS ruled that an LLC could qualify for partnership tax status that its popularity spread. Today 48 states (excluding Vermont and Hawaii) and the District of Columbia have LLC statutes. Although they vary significantly, nearly all statutes provide for limited liability, partnership tax status and operational flexibility. Some state statutes restrict the types of businesses, such as banking, trust and insurance, that may set up an LLC.

In the past years LLC's have replaced many other business structures such as general partnerships, C corporations, S corporations, limited partnerships, and sole proprietorships. The most common is the replacement of limited partnerships, particularly those used to hold and operate real estate investments. In fact, several the partnerships we surveyed had formed LLC's as the named general partner entity. The advantage to the former general partners is that no one needs to assume unlimited liability for partnership debts. The advantage to the former limited partners is that they may manage the LLC themselves or create an operating agreement with a manager and retain more control over management than they had under a limited partnership agreement. Some investors would discount this advantage and say that the amount of control allowed for limited partners is adequate especially under the newer Revised Uniform Limited Partnership Act that has been adopted, at least in part, in most states. The former limited partners may also prefer LLC's to limited partnerships because of the flexibility in dividing profits that do not need to be allocated in proportion to the members' capital contribution.

Some disadvantages in utilizing an LLC for private equity investments by nontaxable public entities have been expressed. First, the documentation of the structure is thought to be unnecessarily complicated and not worth the effort since a major advantage of the LLC is favorable tax treatment, a matter of little concern to public fund investors. Second, LLC's are a relatively new legal entity without sufficient case law to give confidence to the investors that exercising their rights under an operating agreement will not trigger some sort of liability. Third, investors are not sure how the operating agreement will be a useful mechanism to increase their control over management when numerous other investors are involved as members. Fourth, some investors do not like the idea that general partners can cover themselves in a cloak of limited liability in the LLC structure. They believe this reduces their accountability to the other investors.

Another issue involving LLC's centers around the question of whether the interests are securities. There is no clear answer on this yet. By way of analogy, if a business owner sells his or her interest in a business that depends upon his or her efforts to make a profit, the interest is not considered a security. However, if a person invests in a business with the expectation of making profits solely through the efforts of others, courts usually treat that as a security.

California is one state which has said that in an LLC where all members actively participate in the business, the membership interests will not be treated as securities under its state law.

In summary, LLC's are worth watching as legal developments unfold and case law precedents are established. Some large investorss may seek to pursue private equity investments under a LLC structure. We would not be surprised to see such a vehicle being offered to investors soon.

Compensation of General Partners

Compensation broadly covers the overall remuneration and benefits paid to individuals. General partner compensation packages typically include a base salary, carried interest sharing and often include perquisites such as company cars, club memberships, personal financial planning services, cellular phones, etc. While some of these may sound excessive, they are consistent within the private equity industry as well as with senior level managers in high growth industries.

Many large investors have adopted a common notion of "pay for performance." In the public equities markets, some public funds strongly advocate shareholder activism in rewarding senior company management only if shareholder wealth is generated. At the portfolio level, the debate between active and passive management of public equities is often analyzed on an after-fee basis. Where excess returns cannot be generated using active managers, passive funds are favored.

The "pay for performance" approach is clearly extending into the private equity arena. Investors believe that the compensation structure of general partners represents an alignment of interests. Attempts by investors to obtain disclosure on compensation are either rebuffed or the details provided are sparse. Budget-based fees are a way for investors to obtain compensation related information as well as to have an effective mechanism to manage overall costs. The linkage of compensation explains part of the heavy resistance by general partners against budget-based fees.

General partners argue that investors' concerns with compensation are unimportant. They point to strong performance records to justify their level of fees. However, it is really the base salary component of compensation where investors focus their attention as an alignment of interest issue. The base salary is heavily influenced by and linked to the management fee received. For example, if a flat management fee of 2% on committed capital is contractually agreed upon for the term of the partnership. While this may create an incentive for a general partner to remain at the firm, an excessive base salary raises concern that the effort level will be diminished.

Notwithstanding full disclosure by the general partners, the salary component of compensation that an average general partner receives may be roughly approximated. We estimate that the general partner salary expense tends to be 30% to 60% as a percentage of total operating expenses. The smaller percentage will apply to larger general partnerships whereas the larger percentage applies to smaller or newly established general partnerships. As an example, a partnership consisting of five general partners that has raised $300 million in committed capital with a 2% management fee will have an annual general partner salary expense of $1.8 million (30% of 2% of $300 million), or approximately $360,000 on average per general partner. This method will not provide insight into the distribution of salaries, and the range can be quite wide, but it may be helpful for investors in assessing the salary/alignment of interests issue. While this measure may result in some high salaries with respect to other professions, it may be helpful as a comparative measure within the private equity industry.

Investment Guidelines

A general partner usually has freedom to invest in deals it feels are appropriate. While it is unusual to see significant deviations from what the general partners said they were going to set out to do, it is possible that this can occur. The temptation may arise to invest in a bigger deal and expose the partnership to a higher degree of risk. This situation may also trigger a potential conflict of interest if general partners also co-invest. Another situation that would be of concern to a number of public funds is a politically or socially incorrect investment.

The partnership agreement should contain investment guidelines for diversification and investment selection. Limited partners should also share any statutory investment restrictions with general partners. While disclosure of this information may not necessarily restrict general partners, it would be a useful input for them when assessing the return potential of a questionable investment. If an investment opportunity arises that would cause the diversification guidelines to be exceeded, then the advisory board should be called in to address the issue.

Oversubscription

Oversubscription occurs when demand for a particular partnership being formed is high and the original subscription amount is exceeded by number of investors awaiting to be limited partners.

General partners have four choices when oversubscription occurs:

- exclude the last subscribers;
- exclude subscribers at their own discretion;
- reduce the amount of money each subscriber can invest to accommodate the oversubscription; or
- increase the subscription amount to accommodate all investors.

Points for Consideration

Investors should request a formal disclosure of the general partner's procedures if oversubscription occurs. This assures no unpleasant surprises if there an oversubscription situation occurs.

Early subscribers would probably be most satisfied with the first option where later subscribers would be closed out. Exclusion of subscribers at the general partner's discretion is not a democratic process and it would benefit investors to know beforehand that this possibility might occur.

The effect of reduction of the amount each subscriber can invest will depend on the amount and/or who the later investors are. Ideally, it would be helpful to have an oversubscription process which enables the early subscribers to vote on this issue.

Investors should be concerned with an increase in subscription size that is excessive. It may be more difficult to put a larger amount of capital to work given the partnership's strategy. Consequently, potential returns may be reduced as a result.

Placement Agents

Placement agents play a marketing role during the fund-raising effort by general partners. Placement agents may also play an ongoing role in client servicing.

Fees are generally paid to placement agents from the general partnership and can be a substantial percentage of the management fee. Placement agents also may receive a share of the carried interest.

Points for Consideration

Placement agents play a useful role for the small to medium size or newly formed partnerships as well as smaller- and medium-sized investment funds.

Small, medium or newly formed partnerships may have difficulty raising funds and placement agents play a valuable matchmaking and servicing role. Additionally, smaller- and medium-sized investment funds may not attract the quality or level of interest from partnerships during the fund-raising process. Good placement agents play a valuable role in this regard by screening and matching investment needs to the available set of partnerships raising funds.

Large partnerships and large investment funds find less need for placement agents. All large, established partnerships we surveyed found little or no need for the involvement of placement agents. Large funds typically have investment staffs and private equity consultants evaluating partnership opportunities. The large funds, especially public ones, must give each partnership which solicits it a fair evaluation. Most have established criteria for screening out funds which may be inappropriate for consideration.

The investment staffs at the large public funds we spoke with did not perceive placement agents to be particularly beneficial beyond an introductory capacity and unnecessary for established partnerships. While the fee arrangement between the placement agent and the general partnership is negotiated between themselves, it is a cost that is ultimately borne by the investor. Therefore, when a placement agent is used, it would be useful for investors to know how the agent will be compensated. A general partnership's reliance on placement agents and excessive compensation to agents may to questions regarding the abilities of that partnership.

Target Investment Allocation

The target investment allocation refers to the percentage of total assets that an investor will dedicate to private equities. Given the current level of supply and demand, for a large public fund, it may be impossible to ever reach their stated target. It takes several years before a partnership is fully invested. Since the stock and bond markets have risen strongly, the amount of money needed to be invested with private equity to meet the target have increased substantially. Also, money is returned to investors as investments are liquidated, further reducing the allocation.

Large investors should use the invested capital amount versus committed capital in computing their target investment allocation. This requires a substantially higher capital commitment. Some estimations, based on past performance results suggest that for a large investor, to meet a target invested capital percentage, a committed capital amount of roughly twice the target percentage should be made. For example, to have an invested capital amount of 5% of total assets, a committed capital amount of 10% of total assets should be made.

IV. CLOSING COMMENTS

Private equity investing is not for the simple investor and requires a deep commitment of time and other resources. Private equity investors should be knowledgeable about the terminology, practices, and potential risk and returns. This study attempts to define the key terms and conditions in private equity investing and offers specific suggestions to negotiate a better agreement. The recommendations are not absolute, but as private equity participants consider and incorporate some of these into their investment processes, the industry will be enhanced.

Today's "standards" will ebb and flow with market conditions and supply and demand forces. A prudent investor in the private equity markets will keep sight of the changes that occur and strive to improve their knowledge of best practices that ultimately lead to higher rewards and lower risk.

In closing, we offer some key principles to keep in mind:

- Understand that being a limited partner investor does not obviate fiduciary responsibilities or prudent investor standards;
- Create the proper incentives (short-term and long-term) for key individuals who are general partners to work for the investors;
- Minimize distractions that prevent the general partner from staying focused on the investments at hand; and
- Recognize the long-term nature of private equity investing and issues which can occur during the initial, middle, and end of the investment's term.

V. PRIVATE EQUITY PARTNERSHIP ANALYSIS MODEL

We have developed two models to allow investors to compare the impact of alternative financial terms and to simulate potential partnership returns.

The first model enables comparison of potential returns for three discrete scenarios.

The second model permits the returns of underlying partnership investments to be forecast using a powerful technique called Monte Carlo simulation. This can be a powerful tool in assessing a partnership's potential by using a general partner's forecast of their distribution of returns for underlying investments made by the partnership. Alternatively, a general partner's actual experience or other assumptions may be used. The model is flexible enough to use a variety of predefined distributions such as the normal distribution, triangular, or even a custom distribution. The second model also includes an extensive help file that allows interactive look-up features for all of the terms and conditions described in this study.

General Assumptions

1. The partnership will invest in two companies per year over a five year investment period.
2. Each company will be held for five years and then exited.
3. Each company will grow in value each year at the specified return rate and the partnership will value each company at this value.
4. Carried interest will occur depending on status of fund at the end of the previous year. For example, if the carried is after a hurdle of 10%, then a carried will be paid in year seven if the LP IRR after year six is greater than or equal to 10%.
5. Management fees are separate from committed capital.
6. The partnership will invest in two companies per year over a five-year investment period.
7. Each company will be held for five years and then exited.

Base Case Assumptions

The following are the base case assumptions used in modeling the examples described in the study.

Total Committed	$	300,000,000
Investable		100.00%
Return Company 1		20.00%
Return Company 2		20.00%
Return Company 3		20.00%
Return Company 4		20.00%
Return Company 5		20.00%
Return Company 6		20.00%
Return Company 7		20.00%
Return Company 8		20.00%
Return Company 9		20.00%
Return Company 10		20.00%
Fee Type (flat, budget, sliding)		flat
Flat Fee Rate		2.00%
Other Fee's (amort., etc)	$	100,000
If sliding, fee schedule		
Year 1		2.00%
Year 2		2.00%
Year 3		2.00%
Year 4		2.00%
Year 5		2.00%
Year 6		2.00%
Year 7		1.50%
Year 8		1.50%
Year 9		1.00%
Year 10		1.00%
Investment Banking Fee		1.50%
Break-Up Fee's		0.00%
Board Fee's	$	-
Directors Options	$	-
Fee Sharing (pro-rata,%)		50.00%
GP Capital Contribution - %		1.00%
Carried Interest - GP		20.00%
Carry Style (Inv, Capr, Hrdl)		Capr
Hurdle Rate		20.00%
Salary Expense	$	4,000,000
Salary Expense Growth		5.00%
Office Expense	$	200,000
Office Expense Growth		5.00%
Other Expense (travel, etc)	$	150,000
Other Expense Growth		5.00%

Inputs

Our model requires inputs for up to three scenarios for the following variables:

Variable	Choices	Comments
Total committed	Any $	Adjusts the size of the partnership for the user's desired size.
Investable	Any %	Provides ability to adjust for reserves partnerships may require.
Return Company 1-10	Any %	Provides a annual rate of return for each investment.
Fee Type	Flat, Budget, Sliding Scale	Provides toggle between a flat fee on committed capital, budgeted fee on actual expenses, or sliding scale over the life of the partnership.
Flat Fee Rate	Any %	If flat fee is in effect, then this field provides the rate of that fee.
Other Fees (amort., etc.)	Any %	Provides the ability to adjust for other fees outside of the management fee. Places the amount in each year of the partnership's life. Examples may include amortization of organizational expense or other such fees.
Investment Banking Fee	Any %	Fee charged on origination of each deal during investment period.
Break-up Fees	Any %	Fee charged on broken deals. During investment period uses percentage of money put to work.
Board Fees	Any $	Compensation received for sitting on boards. Multiplies this amount by number of investments held. Amount should be average compensation from board seats per investment.
Directors' Options	Any $	Compensation received as part of director's incentive. Paid in final 5 years in model.
Fee Sharing	Pro-rata, Any %	Sharing of extra fees. Pro-rata divides fee in proportion to capital contribution. Percentage is amount of fees which would go to limited partners.
GP Capital Contribution	Any %	Percentage of total capital contributed by general partner in the same terms and conditions of limited partners.
Carried Interest	Any %	Percentage of gains which are given to general partner for incentive.
Carry Style	Inv, Capr, Hrdl	Style of carried interest calculation. "Inv" is a carried interest on each investment (deal-by-deal). "Capr" is a carried interest after

		capital is returned to limited partners (aggregation). "Hrdl" is a carried interest after a hurdle rate is achieved.
Hurdle Rate	Any %	If hurdle rate carriy style is chosen, this percentage is the hurdle.

Inputs

Variable	Choices	Comments
Salary Expense	Any $	Total payroll of general partner. Used to calculate budget fee and also compare to flat rate management fees.
Salary Expense Growth	Any %	Grows salary annually at specified rate in order to compensate for growing staffs, raises, inflation, etc.
Office Expense	Any $	Total facilities expense of general partner. Used to create budget fee and also compare to flat rate management fee.
Office Expense Growth	Any %	Grows office expense annually at specified rate in order to compensate for adding offices, increasing rents, inflation, etc.
Other Expense (travel, etc.)	Any $	Total other expenses of general partner such as travel, postage, etc. Used to create budget fee and also compare to flat rate management fee.
Other Expense Growth	Any %	Grows other expense annually at specified rate in order to compensate for effects of changing environment of general partner.
Net LP IRR	Calculated Field	Provides limited partner net-IRR given the specified variable terms.

Output

The output lists all inputs for three discrete scenarios and the resultant output. Detailed spreadsheets for all cash flows are provided as well as two graphs showing the annualized and cumulative net-IRR to limited partners (J-curves). Once the simulation is completed, a detailed report which summarizes the simulation results including statistics and percentile analysis. Year-by-year net-IRR to limited partner is shown as well as for the entire term of the partnership.

Methodology

The study included our collective experience and expertise in the private equity market along with input collected from knowledgeable parties: limited partners, consultants, attorneys, and general partners. We felt that the interests of all parties, including general partners, needed to be considered for us to develop realistic rather than merely idealistic suggestions.

The basic premise underlying our approach was that general partners will attempt to negotiate terms and conditions that the market will bear. If the markets' investors are more knowledgeable about the best practices and most favorable terms, then negotiations should proceed in a quicker, more professional fashion and result in a better contract.

The specific steps of the study are described as follows:

Survey of Sponsoring Public Fund Perceptions

The initial step entailed interviewing senior investment representatives from state funds. Interviewees were either the Chief Investment Officer, Senior Private Equity Investment Officer, or both. The interviews provided us with experiences, concerns and expectations of these public funds in the private equity market.

The first step also included the development of a questionnaire which was completed by private equity investment specialists. Responses to the questionnaire confirmed what we had identified as the key issues, terms and conditions affecting private equity investors. Copies of private equity contracts were also supplied by the public funds and analyzed by us in this step. The contracts represented a cross section of private equity funds including, venture capital and leveraged buyout.

Survey of Private Equity Consultants and Legal Counsel

The objective of the second step was to obtain input from other experts who assist the sponsoring state public funds. We focused on issues, terms and conditions highlighted from the first step and developed questionnaires that solicited their input on these items and on the suggestions, we were considering.

To identify the key issues and contractual provisions to be analyzed, we developed questionnaires for alternative investment consultants and attorneys used by the sponsoring public funds. These questionnaires focused on terms and conditions we considered to be key in impacting risk and returns.

Development of Points for Consideration

The first three steps framed the areas where we would be most helpful. Our efforts were then focused on identifying and recommending best practices and developing points for consideration by investors.

Return Analysis Model

We have developed a useful model for analyzing returns with alternative contractual terms and we decided to use it as a basis for our model. The model allows discrete analysis of the net-IRR to limited partners when various assumptions about individual deal returns and contractual terms are modified. Our model further builds upon this by including:

- an analytical module to compare three different contractual term scenarios

- a simulation module to stochastically model distributions of individual deal returns

- a user-friendly interface to control inputs and view outputs

- an extensive interactive "help feature" to enable users to look up definitions, list the various practices that have been used for structuring contractual terms and identify recommended best practices

Where possible, we used the model to quantify and illustrate our suggestions described in this guide. The model and its assumptions are described in section V.